THE AUTOBIOGRAPHY

OF

THE "SARK" M.P.

The entire profit of this book will be devoted to the debt on the Children's Ward of the Cumberland Infirmary.

JOHN HEYWOOD LTD.

PRINTERS AND PUBLISHERS, MANCHESTER AND LONDON.

This book is dedicated to my brother David,
who endured more patience with me that any
other man either could or would during the years
of our partnership.

CONTENTS.

———

Oh, that mine enemy would write a book.

The evil that men do lives after them ; the good is often buried with their bones.

INTRODUCTORY.

IN attempting to write a book I make no claim to literary attainments. I am a busy man, and have not time for calm thought and reflection. My articles in the " East Cumberland News," Carlisle, have been widely read. Some people tell me that they have derived amusement from them, and others tell me they have derived some help ; others say the writer must be a bit deranged. I cannot please everybody, so I don't try. The lessons contained herein have been obtained in the hard battle of life. I am responsible for no man's opinions. I simply state my own. Many people may think I have dealt too heavily in my own photos. A traveller once wanted to show his samples, but was refused permission to do so ; when he said he wanted to see them himself. That is one reason why I have borrowed them from friends. I believe in patronising local industries. I have got my book printed in Manchester, as I don't want any reflections passed on a local printer. I have a blunt and abrupt way of expressing myself. My bluntness and abruptness might not help the reputation of a Carlisle printer. I am not a proud, vain, or rich man. I believe I am the man who, amid a strenuous life, has given more time and money to help some " pairts " of Cumberland than any other Cumberland man during the last 21 years. I ask all my constituents to be like a hen amongst chaff : Pick out the bits of grain and don't bother about the chaff.

Carlisle, April, 1910.

MY TRADE MARK.

Photo by   K. Moffitt, Accrington & Burnley.

Yours heartily
The "Sark" M.P.

Photo by   Scott & Son, Carlisle.

MY FATHER.

Photo by   Scott & Son, Carlisle.

MY MOTHER.

Photo by   *Scott & Son, Carlisle.*

As I Went to the "Sark" Trade.

AGE 15½ YEARS.

Photo by   Scott & Son, Carlisle.

AGE 19 YEARS.

As Member First Manchester Volunteers.
Age 22 Years.

Photo by   Lafosse, Manchester.

AGE 22 YEARS.

AGE 27 YEARS.

Photo by   Vandyke, Liverpco!.

AGE 28 YEARS.

B

Photo by   Scott & Son, Carlisle.

AGE 36 YEARS.

Photo by   R. Moffitt, Accrington & Burnley.

AS CAPTAIN.   AGE 42 YEARS.

Photo by   *R. Moffitt, Accrington & Burnley.*

AGE 47 YEARS.

Photo by   R. Moffitt, Accrington & Burnley.

AGE 58 YEARS.

Photo by   R. Moffitt, Accrington & Burnley.

AGE 58 YEARS.

Photo by MYSELF AND FAMILY, Including Poor "Vick," who Died Nov. 28th, 1909. F. Heyworth, St. Annes

THE "SARK" M.P.

CHAPTER I.

MY EARLY DAYS.

I WAS born in the village of Hethersgill on January 29th, 1852, and was one of a family of eleven children, eight of whom still survive. Without exaggeration, I can truly say no family have descended from better parentage. Taking the limitation of his environment into consideration, I have yet to meet my father's equal. In form and features he bore a striking resemblance to the late William Ewart Gladstone, and was on several occasions mistaken for him. In spirit he also possessed many of the noble qualities of the great statesman. I once heard the Rev. Samuel Chadwick say that his mother possessed more commonsense to the square inch than any woman he had ever met. I can say the same thing. No wife ever looked better to the ways of her household, and her children have risen up to call her blessed. My father was an impulsive man; I have inherited that useful characteristic. There are any amount of men in the world who are steadfast and immovable; the Apostle Peter was an impulsive man, but he came in useful at certain periods. He did things that none of the other apostles dare tackle, and, of course, he sometimes did things that would have been better left alone. The man who made no blunders in the Apostolic Age was not much use, nor are they much good in this strenuous age. There is still room for an odd Peter or two. My mother was a woman who possessed her soul in patience; a most useful trait in any one's character.

I must confess I have not taken after my mother in that particular phase of human nature. I infer that the stock of an impulsive father and a patient mother, given some chance to start life, should be of some use in life. So if the " Sark, M.P.," is not a decent kind of chap, he ought to be. The so-called Upper Ten may look down on the village cottage homes, but they really ought to look up to them. What does England possess to-day that has not emanated from the men who have been born in the humblest homes in our land ? Were the men who invented locomotive engines, pumping engines, mill machinery, etc., born in our stately mansions ? To what class of men does England owe her supremacy in the rank of nations, and made her mistress of the seas ? Is there any need for creeping and cringing to the so-called aristocratic section of our communities ? Bobby Burns said an " Honest man is the noblest work of God." If that statement was true, then my father took rank in the noblest section of our population, and was one of earth's purest and best aristocrats.

During the years my parents lived in Hethersgill few villages could compare with it for the quality of its inhabitants. I can still look back and catch inspiration from the noble, upright, and unselfish lives of the people that surrounded my parents' cottage. All the old folks, but one, have passed away. To-day Hethersgill will stand comparison with most villages for kindly decent folks ; but I can truly say, without any insult to them, or without meaning any offence, the quality has gone down a bit. This fact is easily accounted for. The grasping spirit of our day has contaminated our villages as well as our towns. As far as moral tone is concerned, I was born under wealthy conditions. The village lad who has to push and fight his way in the world, starts well equipped for his work if under similar conditions. It will easily be seen that a small nest with eleven chickens in it will soon get too small for its brood ; some of the birds must tumble out or get pushed out. So as each chicken got big enough we had to leave the old nest and go and try to pick a bit of food further afield. My father began and finished his education in three months. He was the best writer of a word and the worst hand at spelling a word I ever knew. Feeling his early disadvantages, he tried to remedy them in his off-

Photo by   Farrer, Wetheral.

THE COTTAGE WHEREIN I WAS BORN.

spring. He did the best his circumstances would allow, and angels cannot beat that.

My father was a country joiner. He built carts, coffins, farmhouses, or anything else that wanted building. In a comparatively poor agricultural district a man had to be competent to turn his hand to anything that turned up. The standard wage for a day's work was 2s. 6d. and food ; so 15s. is not an extravagant amount to support a large family. My father was " King of his own castle." After many years of patient plodding labour and self-denial, they got the cottage, wherein I was born, free from debt. He usually kept two pigs and a cow. My mother and I generally put the garden square ; so with what country joinering and a large garden, orchard, and our farm stock produced, his family lived decently ; and through the help of my mother's care and skilful management we always cut as respectable appearance as some families whose financial conditions were more fluent. We were a happy family. My father played a clarionet, and on Sunday nights we had a family concert. My six sisters had all good voices, so a good two hours' exercise of their vocal powers enabled us all to enjoy a plain and nutritious supper.

I am glad I was one of a large family. The large families of poor parents have, and are still, one of the most valuable assets of our national life. Five of my sisters were older than me, and they had all departed to seek fresh fields and pastures new. Then my turn came to leave the old nest. My father had a friend who had prospered in the drapery trade, who told him to make Will a draper, and I'll see him alright. My father, being anxious that my lot in life should be easier than his had been, apprenticed me to a draper in Brampton. I had to live indoors, and was supposed to get a sufficient supply of food as my natural body required. What a gruesome tale could be told or written of the luxuries supplied to indoor drapery apprentices in Cumberland, London, and other places ! My articles in the " East Cumberland News " have thrown some light on the glorious retail drapery trade. The miserable five years dragged their weary length along, but everything has an end, except a suet pudding, which has two. There are a few decent drapers, but the majority of them are contemptible men, who live and die to scrape money together. Brampton drapers were mostly no better than their brethren in most places. Going as a small lad, at 15¾ years of age, I set off growing, and in a few years assumed the physical proportions of a respectable fishing-rod. What a number of decent villagers' sons have been thrown into consumption and brought to a premature end through poor food and long fasts! My penal servitude came to an end. The friend of my father had collapsed through over work. I was thrown on my beam ends. Several of my sisters being located in Manchester, I naturally turned my gaze to Cottonopolis. I left Brampton with a frame without flesh on it. I left the city without any letters of introduction in my pocket to the firms my master had done business with. Lots of people say and think there is no hell. If there is not, there ought to be one. The mercenary wretch who can keep decent people's lads for five years, and who do not help those lads to get a start in life, ought to be put in a real hot one. After a fortnight's stay at home, I set off to seek my fortune in Manchester with no influence at my back. God help the lad who has to face Manchester with a lean frame and no friends. I travelled Manchester's weary streets for six weeks, and got work at last at the immense salary of £25 a year with food. What a glorious start in financial remuneration! What a splendid opportunity I had to recoup my parents for the five years strain they had passed through to get me initiated into some of the mysteries of the glorious trade of a retail draper! The splendid conditions described are not defunct yet in the same wonderful city. It is only a short time since I had to give a Kirklinton lad a push up, who went to Manchester under as favourable conditions as I entered it. When I left Hethersgill I was nearly 21, so my early days being accomplished I must weave the sequel of them into my future chapters.

R. B. Nicholson, Carlisle.

MY NATIVE VILLAGE, HETHERSGILL.

Photo by

CHAPTER II.

Village Methodism.

ALTHOUGH I have spent the greatest part of my business life in or near Manchester, and have been associated with Old Gravel Lane Chapel for a good slice of that time, my sympathies have always travelled in the direction of our neglected out-of-the-way villages. To what extent I am indebted to the influence of Old Nether House Chapel, I cannot form a just estimate. My father was brought up in connection with the Church of England. Like a good many others, he was a useless member of it. It is supposed to be a little higher in the social scale to be an attendant at a church rather than a humble little barn-like structure, of which I now furnish my readers with an example. Before going an inch further let me state emphatically that I have no sectarian animosity to the Established Church, I think I have as many friends as most folks, and I am glad to state that many of my best friends are Church people. One of the most painful phases of country life, to me, is the apparent lack of Christian love, which ought to exist amongst different sects ; I am fairly sick of sects, creeds, and dogmas. Tennyson said " There is more faith in honest doubt than in half the creeds." Both sides are to blame where animosity or sectarian difference exist. I am quite sure Wesleyan Methodism has had an uplifting influence in our national life. I am also quite certain that if Methodists had gone on in the spirit of early Methodism the sordid greed and grab for wealth, that obtains all over our country, would not have reached the shameful condition it has.

John Wesley predicted that wealth would be the greatest danger to his followers, and in that respect he has been a true prophet. In all country or other districts there is a work for the church and chapel to do. Where no chapel is found, stagnation generally reigns supreme. I am often sorry for the Church of England as found in our rural districts. Plenty of its clergymen have no more idea what genuine religion means than a tom-cat. A clergyman's position is unique in his parish. It is a respectable business. No position in life tends more to indolence and apathy. The parish priest is monarch of all he surveys, either socially, politically, or from any other standpoint. Many of them think theirs is the only correct route to heaven ; that idea is a rotten one. I think the true church is composed of all the true Christians of every sect. I believe a man may have been baptised, confirmed, and take the sacrament regularly, and know practically nothing of true religion. The best test, I think, in judging whether we are religious or not lays in this point : Are you thinking and trying to help others to a better life ? A servant is the real Christian spirit, a " boss " or master is on the wrong lines. Christ came not to be ministered to, but to minister and give his life a ransom for many. Hundreds of church ministers, and many other kinds of ministers, do not worthily earn their salt, let alone their salaries. Don't think that I think all Wesleyan ministers do their duty ; plenty don't. Some have not an ounce of the spirit of John Wesley in them. We have some men who are the bane of our stationing committee ; no circuit wants them, so they are generally pushed on to the country circuits, where there is scarcely anyone to oppose their appointment to it. This is a great mistake. It is the country lads who largely keep the world going ; so I think the best ministers should give a hand in helping to bring out the best assets of our national and religious life. No doubt many of our country rectors and country circuit ministers would do better for their flocks if they got more kind words and more visible signs of appreciation of their labours. Grumblers are often in the ascendancy everywhere. But to come back to Nether House Chapel : As I have stated, my father was a nominal adherent to the church. If we ask the majority of non-church goers we meet to which denomination they belong, they generally avow they are churchmen. Revival missions have always been a special feature in the Methodist church. A young Scotch evangelist came to hold a mission in the Old Chapel ; his earnest manner and evident sincerity drew men to the services who seldom went to any place of worship. Amongst the number was my father. Having never attended a mission service previously, the mode of its procedure strangely impressed him. The evangelist was the first extempore preacher he ever listened to. For the first time in his history he was led to see that religion was a vital matter and of personal importance. That night was the turning point in his history. Impulsive men go more quickly to Christ than those of calm temperament. Conversion in St. Paul's case was quick. Some men and women can mark the spot, remember the date, etc., of their start in entering the Christian warfare ; others, of gentler mould and retiring natures, come gradually into the same fight. My father at once decided to lead a Christian life. My gentle mother did the same, and what my father's first visit to that little, unattractive structure, and the results emanating from that visit, eternity can only reveal. It is righteousness that exalteth a nation, more than large armies and powerful navies. England to-day is great. How much greater would her moral power be if she had transmitted more of the real Christ-like character (which is still her greatest asset) and less of our national vices to her Colonies. We send missionaries abroad, and they are generally the pioneers of civilisation in so-called heathen countries. How often are their labours blighted and hampered by the money-grabbing rascals, who are the curse of our country both at home and abroad. No wonder that half-awakened tribes ask themselves the question : Are these men samples of the Christians in the land from whence their missionary has come ? English visitors to foreign lands are often glib in their condemnations of the work of missionaries. What eloquent tales we have listened to in their recital of the laziness and apathy of the men who are sent out to preach the simple Gospel of Christ ! There may be some missionaries who should never have been missionaries ; but have we not a fair supply of ministers in every denomination in our land who, judging by their efforts and the result of their ministries, seem to have got to the wrong job ? What about David Hill, in China ; William Carey, in India ; Dr. Coke ; John Hunt, who went from the plough-tail in Lincolnshire, and who wore himself out in ten years amongst men-eating cannibals ? Can

c

Photo by.   HETHERSGILL, CHAPEL.   Farrer, Wetheral.

England, to-day, bear comparison to the Fiji Islands ? As righteousness has exalted our nation, so the same spirit elevates the country cottages, farmhouses, and a few of the lordly mansions in our land. A tree is known by its fruit, so the fruit the little mission service produced became visible, and Kirklinton, to-day, still feels a part of the debt of the fruit crop. Throwing in their lot with the little Wesleyan Society at Nether House, my parents became (with all due respect to the other members) its chief asset. My home became the home of the travelling preachers, as the circuit ministers were in those days.

These days of hurry, committee meetings, and the numberless demands of our town societies, have robbed Methodism of one of its greatest and most potent influences. I still remember the visits of the circuit minister to the old homestead. In the monotony of village life, as bairns, how we looked forward to those visits. What a number of country lads have got their first, stimulation to an upward growth in character from the kindly pat on the head and a few kind words from our ministers. I have heard my friend, the late Rev. Thomas Champness, state that they were richer in stock than money in his father's house. The domestic quiver was full of arrows, so was my father's house ; but a bed was always found for the minister, which usually meant some of the youngsters being boarded out for the night. My home was also the home for the local preachers, and for years the only home for the man who often tramped ten miles to preach. The local preacher is often sneered at in these days, but where is the mathematician who can calculate what England owes to the noble army of the Great Unpaid ? Minister and local preacher were always welcome. Did you ever know a man pass through the Bankruptcy Court who gave part of his small income to such hospitality ? The House of Commons, to-day, has many of its best orators who have obtained their eloquence in humble Methodist chapels, and who still continue to exercise their gifts in Dissenting chapel pulpits.

Most of our family being located in or near Manchester, my parents, largely at my suggestion, left the Old Nest and went to live in that wonderful, if dirty, city. What it must have meant to them I cannot gauge, but it was a huge mistake on my part. It is at the wrong end of life to be transplanted. Possessed of more than ordinary vitality, new conditions must have grated on my father's nerves. I can still recall the sight of the drooping frame, once so erect, taking his little grandson, of his own name, to see the engines at Victoria Station. The little grandson is now a man, and the front portrait in this book is a proof of his skill as a photographer. My mother managed to pass the time better, as her industry in the old home found scope in the new. At the time I paid quarterly visits to the old parish when travelling for orders. How my father looked forward to my return. How often we sat until daylight broke through the window shutters, and how he recalled incident after incident of his Hethersgill days. How many times he told me the things over again that I had heard scores of times before ; but I could always listen to the recital without impatience, as our talk seemed to be one of the few earthly pleasures left to him. His end came suddenly. A Cumberland friend called, and in their conversation the old man became unduly excited and passed peacefully away. My mother lived about two years after him, and then rejoined the partner of her joys and sorrows during a journey through life of over fifty years.

I took my father round Kirklinton with me on my second journey. During our chat in driving along he said to me : " Will, there was always something in thy mother, the best I ever saw in a woman."

The day after my father died, my mother and I sat together, and she said : " Well, Will, he's gone, but I never said anything to him that I would like unsaid, and never did anything to him that I would like undone."

I am not a good hand at sitting over graves. A few weeks ago I visited the grave of my parents in Kersal Moor Churchyard, on the outskirts of Manchester. I stood and looked at the three names on the tombstone. The first one being the name of my youngest sister, who was cut off in her prime ; then I gazed at the other two names, and wondered if the offspring of such a noble couple had proved worthy of their parentage. I thought of the male portions of my father's brothers' families. Many of them started life under easier and more favourable financial conditions than I had. Several of them have passed away without leaving many traces of their footprints on the sands of time. If, during a strenuous life, I have tried to make some parts of the world better, what has been the propelling force that has caused me to do it? To-day, financially, I could have been a wealthy man; the ball lay at my feet. If I had backed up my brother David's efforts, we could have swept East Lancashire. If so, what then? Would the sweeping operations have swept some poor struggling draper off his legs, and he and his family into poverty? Is there a Divinity shaping our ends, rough hew them how we will? My parents passed away, as many worthy village Methodists pass away, without any mention of their departure in the Methodist newspapers. Does the noble chapel, standing in our old garden on the site where the gooseberry bushes grew; the lovely Sunday school, now standing on the site of our old piggery; the reading and recreation rooms (once part of the old cottage), equipped in a style that no other Cumberland village reading room is furnished; are they not the outcome of the noble lives of old Wully and Sarah Moffitt?

Should these lines catch the eye of any despondent worker in our neglected villages, I ask can you not catch any inspiration from the portraits I have drawn? Every village society nearly has its little squabbles. My parents were not perfect, but no black looks or unkindly words ever shifted their allegiance to duty. In nearly every village the hard work is done by two or three members. The others are content to grunt and grumble, without doing a sensible stroke of work to make things better. Do your part. No one else can do your work. Try to send out your bairns into the world's rough fight and present them with an example worthy of imitation.

Photo by

R. Moffitt, Accrington & Burnley.

NETHER HOUSE CHAPEL

(WITH REV. DINSDALE T. YOUNG AND LATE H. B. HARRISON, ESQ.)

CHAPTER III.

The Building of Hethersgill Chapel.

The Old Nether House Chapel, having served its day and generation well, began to show internal signs of decay. Few old places have had a better record. Many men and women, now far distant, could testify to the blessings received within its walls. What Sunday-school anniversaries we had! How we all looked forward to the day! It was the red-letter day of the whole year. What wonderful dialogues I took part in! How pathetic were some of our recitations! What irresistible financial appeals issued from the mouth of the boy who was delegated to undertake the collection manifesto! What emotions were stirred by our annual hymn, commencing "Another happy golden year," etc. Even in a thinly populated district some gaps were made in some homes, and some of the bonny bright bairns that joined in the opening song had either left the district or had arrived where gaps in families are unknown. The annual rigout for both little and big bairns took place for the great occasion. Both superintendent, teachers, and scholars were arrayed in the best attire that the slender purses of some of us could procure. How the old chapel was packed once a year at least! Parents who did not go in for much church or chapel going during the other 51 Sundays of the year put in appearance to brighten and adorn the crowd. Kirklinton is not an emotional district, and not many pocket handkerchiefs have to be dried throughout the year, but a few faces got wet at the great annual festival. Of the many wrenches I endured when leaving home, was the fact of missing our Sunday-school anniversary. Sad times still come back to memory. I can still recall a lot of the pieces and dialogues, although my last personal appearance in connection with the school took place 38 years ago.

Where are the friends of my youth ? How widely scattered are those who are still alive. How many have entered into a larger room ? They have not gone from us for ever, as the pathetic ballad puts it. The Sunday services were followed the next day by the usual tea meeting and public service at night. Those tea meetings are still fragrant in my mouth. Didn't we boys go for the well-spread contents of the tea tables ! I can still see my Aunt Mary at her post. She was everybody's Aunt Mary. No tea meeting was complete without her. Sister to my dear old mother ; like my mother, she filled her niche in life well. She was born, lived, and died in the same house, after a sojourn of 88 years. For many years her home was my home in my visits to Kirklinton. Many a time I have looked at her and wondered why she had never been compelled to change her name from Hope to some other one with less attraction in it. Perhaps it was as well, as it is better to be living in hope than dying of despair. It may be some comfort to my many maiden lady friends to know that the best are generally left, even if that be poor consolation. But we must come back to our starting point. No doubt most village chapels in agricultural squandered districts have taken much thought, work, and energy to get them free from debt ; but I think few will be able to compare with the years of strain before Hethersgill Chapel and Sunday School arrived at that satisfactory stage of their existence.

For many years I had lived the life of a nominal member of the Wesleyan Methodist connexion. I was a fair representation of many of its members to-day. I neither helped the Wesleyen body much, but, on the other hand, I did not do it any harm. I was strictly honest in business, and always had as much practical Christianity as to pay my bills. As a travelling draper I put my religion into my patterns. For nearly 20 years I covered the same ground. To-day I could look every customer I ever had business dealings with straight in the face, and I defy any one of them to charge me with a sneaky or dishonest business transaction. That is something to be thankful for, even in the stage of religious apathy I had almost unconsciously got into. Being much out of Manchester my attendances at the class meeting were rare. However, I always squared up once a quarter, and paid the orthodox amount. What would Methodism have done without its class meeting. George Whitfield made bigger onslaughts on the Devil's territory than John Wesley did, but John was the better organiser. The class meeting propped Methodism and gave it stability. John Wesley was not the originator of class meetings. Read the last book in the Old Testament, chapter iii., verses 16 to the finish of the chapter, and you will find I am right.

There are some services in Methodism peculiarly adapted to Methodists. Given a man of commonsense and a fair knowledge of human nature, and also given a number of people who live upright lives, the Methodist class meeting is a bit of heaven on the march to heaven. There is a big outcry at present in our Wesleyan Church about the conditions of membership. There would not be if the above conditions were obtainable. The failure of present-day class meetings largely lies in the almost superhuman task of getting suitable leaders and pure living on the part of the members. I have told many an unconscious lie in Methodist class meetings. My quarterly utterances contained statements that I thought were true, but they were not. I spoke of having to stay at inns and hotels, which I thought was detrimental to religious progress, etc. My class leader was a modest, gentle man, and he corroborated my statements. Can an innkeeper be a Christian ? I say he can. Travellers must have somewhere to sleep, as they cannot perch on a tree over night. I stayed at many inns, but I cannot remember one instance where I was overcharged in my account, and if all my Methodist friends, past and present, lived as upright lives, and conducted their businesses as fair and square, Methodism would have a better flavour in many parts of our land. Many of my Methodist friends stoutly upheld the idea, that no man could be a Christian and sleep on licensed premises. If such is the truth, why do they not make some effort to protect the poor traveller. I am sorry to state my experience in temperance hotels have not always been satisfactory. Many rigid tea-total travellers are driven into licensed hotels.

During my apathetic days I spent a Sunday with my old friend Jack Bell, at Haltwhistle. Jack had turned over a new leaf in life. His chances had not been my chances ; but he was a long way the better man. So I weighed matters up and determined that his example should spur me into a bit of active service in Christian work.

The Devil does not bother lukewarm Christians ; inconsistent men and lukewarm professors are his best sandwich men. I asked myself a few questions, and determined to

JACK BELL, HALTWHISTLE.

try to make the world a bit better in my own groove. My chum of many years standing, Mr. George Teasdale, was then schoolmaster at Shawfoot School. Driving down to Carlisle together we compared notes, and I believe my castigation of my so-called religious life had the effect of making him go in for some self-examination.

Poor Old Nether House Chapel had got dirty in interior and its members a bit " flat," so I wrote and told them we would have a mission when I came back on my next journey, and I wrote to each member to prepare themselves so that we might expect success. Twenty-one years have elapsed since I took part in that mission. For months I got up early in the mornings and tried to make a few sermons. I don't believe in praying for anything until I have answered my own prayers and have done all I can to expect an answer from headquarters. These conditions being fulfilled, then I think we may pray in the right spirit. I told the bairns at Penton, Roadhead, and Roweltown, when I acted for " Father Xmas," that prayer was asking God for something we felt we stood in need of and expected to get it. I think that a good definition of true prayer. If all our prayer meetings were carried out in that spirit they would become popular once more.

I shall never forget the first night's meeting in that wonderful mission. I had had a hard day's travelling in Scaleby. I arrived at the old chapel physically weary. I fully expected to see the chapel full, if it was only through curiosity. I see the interior of the old chapel vividly in mental view yet. At the time of service two young women sat near the door ; four men sat round the stove. All the members were supposed to have been praying for me and the success of the mission. For various lawful and other reasons, only one member was present at the start, John Irving, the organist. It looked like as if no one else was going to put in appearance, so I said we had better commence. I remember giving out my first hymn in the old rostrum, " I have a Saviour, He's pleading in glory." During the hymn singing the people began to drop in. Whatever faults my Kirklinton friends may possess no one can charge them with being slaves to punctuality. Poor things, many of them had to travel long distances on dirty roads on a dark night. Having five nights at my disposal, I had tried to put together five nice little sermons. I thought I ought to make as good an impression as possible, so I led off with what I thought was my best discourse, " Blind Bartimæus." I knew that brevity covers a multitude of shortcomings in a poor preacher, so I took care to get the service over in an hour. What a wonderful sermon that must have been! I had my notes carefully

Photo by   W. J. Tyne, Stockport.

THE LATE REV. THOMAS CHAMPNESS.

prepared. I have the notes still. Rev. Frederick Friend was the circuit minister at the time. Although they crippled my speech, he said they were in proper order. All kinds of male and female evangelists, good, middling, and bad, had conducted missions in Old Nether House Chapel. My predecessor, in the work before me, had strained the penitent form section of his services severely and ignorantly—in fact, he had lost his temper because the people would not answer

Photo by   Warwick Brookes Manchester.

THE LATE H. B. HARRISON, ESQ.
GRAVEL LANE CHAPEL, SALFORD.

his appeals and come forward. I must say I acted sensibly on that point. I told the people not to come forward until they knew what they were coming out for. I told them not to expect all their troubles would be over if they got converted.

I also told them some of their troubles would only begin in earnest if they changed their mode of living. I think everybody who reads my articles in the " East Cumberland News " will give me credit for calling things by their proper names. It is no use calling a spade an aeroplane. I told

Photo by   *Warwick Brookes, Manchester.*

COUNCILLOR J. BROXAP, ESQ., J.P.
MY BIBLE CLASS TEACHER AT GRAVEL LANE CHAPEL, SALFORD.

the people I would be there prompt at 7 and would commence at 7. I discarded the notes of my second sermon and got my wings at liberty. It was a wonderful service. My good old friend, Mr. James Carruthers (who is about the only one left of the old members), told me that it was about the most powerful service he had ever been in. Don't think I take any personal credit. Some of the best men and women on earth were praying for the mission. Men and women that God cannot turn away, as His promises never fail. Amongst the number were : Rev. Thomas Champness, Mr. H. B. Harrison (of Gravel Lane Chapel, Salford), both of whom have now no need to pray, as their prayers have been turned into praise ; the whole of the Gravel Lane Society, which included my old Sunday-school teacher there, Councillor John Broxap, J.P., who still sticks to his post at one of the most famous chapels in Methodism, and is the strongest prop left ; Mrs. Crook, the Bible woman there still ; and a host of others, who were thick with the Lord, as old Sammy Hick used to put it. It was truly a wonderful time. I left home at midnight on the Sunday night previous to the start of the mission. We had a prayer meeting in our kitchen. My father had had a paralytic stroke, which made his speech difficult, but I still hear the sound of words he could scarcely articulate and the voice that had often resounded in prayer, exhortations and song in the old chapel at Nether House ; he tried to make audible requests for God's blessing on the mission. I was worked up and unnerved before leaving Manchester. I had been trying to do work in the slums of the city. I had been grappling with various difficulties which need not be mentioned here. My impulsive temperament made me kick over the traces, so that I jerked out things that would have been better unsaid, but no one could charge me with lack of energy or purity of motive. On one point, I never lost my head. I made no attempt to drag folks from their seats, and allowed no one else to do it. What lots of folks have been driven away from real and practical religion through indiscretion on a missioner's part ! Kirklinton parish is no worse than any other parish for the relish of a bit of gossip, and I certainly gave them plenty of material to talk about.

The mission commenced on the Wednesday evening. I could not get there earlier. Rev. Frederick Friend was, at the time, stationed in the Brampton circuit. I wrote him saying what God had done for me, and that I was going to try and do something to help others into active work, requesting

THE CROWD AT HETHERSGILL CHAPEL OPENING.

Photo by   R.B. Nicholson, Carlisle.

that he would appoint supply at Nether House Chapel on Sunday, March 4th, 1888. Mr. Friend's reply was most refreshing. He said he would do all he could, both before and after the mission, to help and consolidate the work, but said he would have much preferred to co-operate with me on the ground. Some superintendent ministers could have clipped my wings, and even then they would have only been doing their duty. Before a minister allows a man to try to preach he is supposed to know what that man believes or does not believe. I was not an accredited local preacher. I was not even on trial on any circuit plan. I wrote thanking him for his kindness, and asked him to plan himself, and that I would take the services.

Standing in the rostrum on the Friday night I still see the form of one of the best ministers I have ever known coming up the aisle. He came and asked me, " Do you want me yet, Mr. Moffitt ? " I said, " Not yet, Mr. Friend. Sit down there and I'll tell you when your turn comes on."

I forgot myself during the " pairt " of the service which is alloted to an address or sermon, and talked an hour. Poor Mr. Friend ! Over our frugal but nutritious supper I said you have heard some strange things to-night, Mr. Friend. He burst out laughing and had to plead guilty to the truth of my statement. He told me that it did not seem any trouble for me to talk. How many beginners have trembled in the rostrum through the presence of the minister sitting in judgment on their first oratorical flights ! From a nervous standpoint I had overlooked his presence. I arranged that I should act as super during the mission, and that he could take the place of the young minister. I said let me be the chain-horse, Mr. Friend, so that if I kick I wont hit you. We stayed with good old Aunt Mary and my cousin, Alice Smith. Three things still stand out prominently in my memory, viz., the kindness and attention of our hostess, the generosity of the neighbours, and the prayers of Rev. F. Friend. I attended several series of revival services during my boyhood at the old chapel. They generally lasted a fortnight. The first week was generally considered successful if the services got the members warmed up and into fighting trim. The second week was then supposed to be the period for decisions to take place. This mission could only occupy

D

five nights, so we could not afford to give credit to the old
members. Knowing this I had to give them a " crack on the
lug," as we say in Cumberland, at the first service. I knew
two or three of them could offer prayers either by the mile

Photo by   R. Moffitt, Accrington & Burnley.

Mr. GEORGE TEASDALE,

Evangelist, North Cumberland Mission.

or the acre. I told them at the start I would not have the
prayer meetings spoiled by lengthy utterances. Poor things !
I know I hurt some of their feelings ; but they wanted hurting
badly. Why are prayer meetings so unattractive ? Long,

weary, and useless repetitions have killed many of them. My mode of conducting a mission service was truly of a hotch-potch order.

The success of a meeting does not necessarily depend on the efforts alone of the man in the rostrum. Anybody who could sing a solo decently, speak ten minutes sensibly, or pray for something that was really needed, all got the chance to exercise these gifts. My friend, Mr. Teasdale, was a frequent attendant at the meetings. A short time before the mission began I sent him a brief note of not more than six sentences. One of them was fastened on his memory, and was used to his deciding to change his mode of living. We had been good friends for some years, but religion had not occupied much of our quarterly association with each other. On the Saturday evening Mr. Teasdale made us acquainted with his new resolutions. We had three services on Sunday, March 4th, 1888 ; class meeting in the morning, testimony meeting or love feast at 2-30, and a public service at night. Many old Methodists said they had never attended such three services in all their experience. I shall never forget Mr. Teasdale's first class meeting testimony, and I now reproduce " pairt on't " : " My life was like a rudderless sinking ship, at the mercy of the elements, and I drifted hither and thither with every fretful breeze. Now, I'm more like a steamer, having propelling power within, and under the control and guidance of the Divine Spirit." Mr. Friend led the class meeting. I led the testimony money meeting, fixing Mr. Friend up as the last speaker. I often take part in that meeting yet as I recall the scene. I said there was no compulsion for everybody to speak audibly, and that those who wished could stand up and show their colours. I see Aunt Mary rising to her feet once more. We had a copyhead at Shawfoot School, " An empty vessel makes the greatest sound." Never a public speaker, Aunt Mary preached by a pure life and good example, and the world has never been overstocked or had a surfeit of such preaching. At night the chapel was crowded to suffocating point. The raising of Lazarus through the conversion of the schoolmaster brought many to see and hear what was going on. Many of my old schoolmates that I had expected to see earlier on in the week crept in for the last service. The last public service

Photo by   HETHERSGILL SUNDAY SCHOOL.   Farrer, Wetheral.

was partly ruined by numbers. It was almost impossible to breathe. Many good times had been enjoyed in the old chapel. I question whether ever a better Sunday was ever known in it. Although they are 21 years of age, I still treasure a bundle of letters received from both churchpeople and Wesleyans. In days of my gloom and depression I have turned to them to see if my life had been a failure. Was the Primitive Methodist preacher's life a failure whose sermon was largely composed of the word " Look," that God made the humble instrument of turning Charles Haddon Spurgeon's feet into an opposite direction ?

During the evening service, on that memorable day, I asked Mr. Teasdale to stand up and tell the people what he thought of Christ. I hear his manly words yet, which, through the advantage of education, enabled him to express in graphic language. Some of the best of preachers have died without seeing much visible fruit to their labours. Other men had laboured there for many years. Did I enter into their labours ? Many prayers had been uttered in previous years. Many earnest good men and women spent a good part of that day, in far-off distant places, and to whose influence we can attribute the blessings that have emanated and blessed Kirklinton from these homely services. It is neither by might nor by power, but by my Spirit saith the Lord.

Twenty-one years bring many changes. Many have crossed the border line into a larger room. Many are now living in different places in foreign lands. A few who participated in those services still reside where they were then residing. Our good old friend, the Rev. Frederick Friend, retired from the ranks of the active ministry, is resting quietly until the beginning (not the end) of his long life, at Barnard Castle.

I still retain fragrant memories of the help I got from my church friends. I blurted out many things I would not utter to-day, but no one heard me say one disrespectful word about any other denomination. During the last 21 years I have made repeated efforts in Kirklinton to try and see if I could get church and chapel people to worship God together, but without much success. Will the day ever come that will see the pulling down of sectarian hedges and produce the kindly feeling which will provoke the remark,

Photo by   R. B. Nicholson, Carlisle.

KIRKLINTON PARISH CHURCH.

" See how those different sects of Christians love one another ? " I'm afraid that day is still far distant. The country rector has an inward conviction that Methodists are Schismatics. He labours under the ignorant idea that he is the only man to point people in the right direction. He often asserts that taking the sacrament purges the soul. What rot ! I know plenty men who take the sacrament regularly, who would rob Christ of a threepenny piece before 8 o'clock on Monday mornings. I know men who say they are Unitarians, but they live Christ-like lives. I know Catholics who put the mother of Christ first, but they lead upright, honourable lives, and pay their bills. I know Swedenborgians who say we shall go on in heaven pretty much the same as we are doing now. To me that is not helpful, as I have already had enough of drapers' shops ; but these people have tolerant views and kindly actions. All will come right in the end, as grand old Thomas Guthrie used to assert. I think true religion means self-sacrifice. I think there is nothing to beat a bit of old Methodism. I think if John Wesley were here to-day he would remodel some of his methods ; a bit of commonsense is a grand adjuster.

I had to leave Nether House just at the time I ought to have " stopped on " a bit. George Teasdale and I had been close friends before the mission, but now new ties of friendship had sprung up. At that time George Teasdale was a nominal adherent of the Church of England. When we parted I said, " Never mind about sects, the Lord will guide you. Start at once to visit the sick, people are laying dying like rotten sheep, and no one to go near them." The last night I was there we visited the " Hethersgill Inn." Poor Willie Hope was fast passing away. We scored on that point. The Rector did not know he was dying. He ought to have known. If the Squire at Kirklinton Hall had been dying, would he have been ignorant of the fact ? During the mission I had given some hard knocks. The man who deals out hard blows must expect hard shots back. I got them. To-day my bundle of letters contain epistles I have never seen excelled for the double distilled essence of sarcasm. The composer and copiers of these letters have passed away. All the people who excelled in rancour and condemnation of the mission are resting beneath the green turf. Death

Photo by

HETHERSGILL CHURCH.

R. B. Nicholson, Carlisle.

kills a lot of sectarian bigotry. Death is the only remedy, sometimes, to heal quarrels and break down barriers. Will death ever kill sectarian prejudice ?

The outcome of this mission brought into existence what is now known as the " North Cumberland Mission." A few of the existing members really started it. I developed it. In the meantime I had come into contact with the Rev. Thos. Champness, one of the grandest men that Methodism has produced. He had more heart than head. As the cheapest source of help, I applied to him for an evangelist to work in the district. Poor stuff is always dear at any price. I think we had five samples of Joyful News' Evangelists ; I think I may say most of them had got into the wrong sphere of life. It is a terrible mistake to think that anything will do for a country circuit or a country evangelist anxious to help the outlying districts. I got on wrong lines, so did my dear old friend, Thomas Champness. He had a few good men. He had a good many poor ones ; but he started the " Joyful News' Mission," and Rev. Thomas Cook and Rev. Samuel Chadwick are now supplying what our lamented friend lacked, in turning out men equipped for the arduous and commonsense work of evangelists. Weary of apprentices, I saw the work wanted a journey-man. The right man lay just under my nose. Mr. George Teasdale had now joined the Wesleyan denomination.

Shawfoot School was built by Kirklinton parish money, and not by Church of England cash. The Rector, possessed of secratian views, got it proclaimed as a Church of England School. This gave him the chance to push narrow secratian views. What has produced more rancour, hate, and mischief than political and so-called religious views. The bitterest feuds and most bloody and revolting wars have been created by so-called religious opinions. Mr. George Teasdale was a man. So he should have been. Mr. George Teasdale's mother, like my mother, was one of the salt of the earth. When she departed she left nothing superior in the shape of motherhood, and joined nothing better in the larger edition of life. There ought to be something in hereditary. When the Parish School got under priestly influence the Rector did his best to push rubbish into the minds of the scholars that the scholars' schoolmaster could not swallow or digest.

Knowing the state of affairs, I asked Mr. Teasdale to undertake the work of the North Cumberland Mission. I said, " Weigh matters up, you may give up a certainty for an uncertainty." After serious thought, prayer, and reflection, my son in the Gospel appeared as evangelist of the North Cumberland Mission. Was it a mistake on his part ? Have the weary country tramps, in sick visiting, etc., been an equivalent to the scholastic groove ? Have the visits to the sick and dying made up for educational grants ? We must wait. Things are not what they seem, but all will come right in the end. The Mission kept developing. Other places were added to the list of mission stations.

Nether House Chapel kept going down in its requirements for the parish. The village, not the road-side is the place to concentrate. Through Methodistic influence the top end of the parish had become the most attractive end of the parish for Church of England exertions. Mr. Teasdale put the position before me. The old chapel seemed to have served its purpose. Things internal did not help Methodist influence. Most country chapels have adverse influences to battle with. Most country Methodists take every word they hear for gospel. The old chapel seemed to waver between a revival one week and a little row the next. The environment had changed. Some of the old members had lived and died in thatched cottages. The sons of the old members were living in comparative mansions. Many more thought the old chapel should do. The same men had different views about their private residences. The Kingdom of Heaven is within you. I have stated the fact that the best meetings I ever attended were in kitchens, etc.

Methodism had done well for Kirklinton. What would Kirklinton have been to-day if void of Methodism ? The time had come to rise and build and get into a larger room. I spent three days with Mr. Teasdale looking round the district for a chapel site. I did not want to go so near the church. I respected the feelings of my church friends, and did not want to show any spirit of opposition or sectarian bigotry ; but you have to buy land where it is to be bought. Men possessed of land that should never have been their property would not " pairt " with an inch. I had scarcely returned from my fruitless search to Manchester until the

idea was sprung upon me to try and buy the old cottage
I was born in, and get hold of the garden for a chapel and
Sunday school site. The owners were disposed to sell,
so the bargain was clenched. Once more the old homestead,

Photo by   *Walter Scott, Bradford.*

REV. JOHN HORNABROOKE.

(PRESIDENT-ELECT WESLEYAN CONFERENCE.)

that had cost my father and mother years of strict economy
to get free from debt, came back to one of the family. The
foundation stones of the new chapel were laid on August

16th, 1900. Revs. Thomas Waugh, Thomas Dargue, and Robert Sutton took part in the ceremony. E. Westmorland, Esq., took the chair. We shall draw the curtain over the

Photo by   *R. Moffitt, Accrington & Burnley.*

REV. DINSDALE T. YOUNG.

efforts to put the chapel free from debt. I expected £800 would produce all the place needed. We finished at close on £1,400. The least said is the soonest mended, so the less said about its erection the better. My grand old father would never tolerate debt. I have caught that noble trait in his character. What the Hethersgill chapel has cost me I shall never be able to estimate. Has it been worth the trouble ? Perhaps it has. Few men possess the gift of begging that I have possessed. Has my ingenuity to concoct money-raising for a chapel debt not developed my knowledge of human nature ? Have 5s. appeals, sheep schemes, etc., etc., not brought out some points of character that my character would have been void of to-day ? The chapel was opened the following June. My friend, Rev. H. M. Nield, was the preacher. Have we all forgot the opening sermon on the " Loaves and Fishes " ? The first chapel anniversary sermon was preached by the Rev. John Hornabrooke, General Chapel Secretary and Secretary of the Conference. Some of us still remember his sermon on " Have faith in God." As President of the Conference, Mr. Hornabrooke will preach twice at Hethersgill on Thursday, September 29th. In looking over my long list of contributors, how many have passed away ? Mr. Robert Beaty has gone. Mr. Wm. Beaty has departed ; without Beaty Brothers the North Cumberland Mission and Hethersgill Chapel would have had hard times financially. What does this Mission mean ? Did my friend, Mr. Teasdale, make a mistake in wrecking a scholastic career ? What mean these stones ? Have six years of nervous debility and the blighting of a promising commercial career been too big a price to pay for them ? We must wait until the clouds break and the shadows flee away.

Porthouse, Carlisle.

Photo by   OPENING OF HETHERSGILL READING ROOM.

CHAPTER IV.

THE OPENING OF HETHERSGILL READING ROOM.

EVERYTHING comes to an end in this world. Even a chapel debt can become a thing of the past. The writing of these reminiscences has disinterred many things that happened during the years of strain in getting the debt off. I have been looking at the book which still records my long list of subscribers. It is like a young dictionary. A Scotchman was once asked to look at a new dictionary, and on being asked his opinion of it, he said, " They were very nice stories, but unco short." How often the same names appear at different stages of our efforts! Many names reached the fourth edition, and one the fifth. How well I remember the Saturday morning, when on my way to Carlisle, the postman handed me a letter containing the halves of six five-pound notes from W. Walker, Esq., Whitehaven, to complete the debt. What sad memories crop up in going over the names! How many of them have gone beyond the reach of chapel building appeals! I got sums ranging from 1s. to £100. My list of names include R. W. Perks, Esq., Lord Wolverhampton (then Sir Henry Fowler), T. H. Bambridge, Esq., Beaty Bros., and a host of others. The late Thos. Walker, Esq., Bolton, often helped me to carry my chain. When we had exhausted (as we thought), every available source, how his cheque for £25 put new life into me! Few men will be more missed. A good case always produced a leaf from his cheque book.

My 5s. appeal idea caught on splendidly; I posted 548 one day. Most of them contained a short note in addition to my pictures of the old and new chapels. One more reference I must make before we go on to open the reading room. The financial efforts in connection with Roweltown and Hethersgill chapels brought four bazaars into being. Kirklinton has

MY "SARK" PARADE.—STOPPED BY THE CIVIC AUTHORITIES.

Photo by
Porthouse, Carlisle.

been singularly unfortunate in possessing men to whom we could appeal for personal and financial help. Nor do the prospects in that direction show any signs of improvement. Grab, not give, is still the order of the day. What has been Kirklinton's loss has been Scaleby's gain. R. A. Allison, Esq., has had to stop every gap. Getting out of debt has had one disadvantage, it has robbed me of my chance to borrow help from the adjoining parish. Still possessing " pairt " of the " East Cumberland News " for October 8th, 1908, I now reproduce the cutting. How different would be the social and religious state of our rural districts if their squires imbibed the noble sentiments contained in this paragraph !—

" Mr. Moffitt, in introducing the High Sheriff, said they were very grateful to Mr. Allison for consenting to open the bazaar. He (Mr. Moffitt) thought this was the fourth bazaar that he had had something to do with that Mr. Allison had opened. Mr. Allison had been their never-failing friend. He had always helped them liberally, not only in a financial sense, but also by practical sympathy and in other ways.

" The High Sheriff, who was heartily received, said it was a great pleasure to him to come there and open that bazaar. He knew he had officiated at previous bazaar openings in that district, but was not aware that this was the fourth. There was a limitation to one's capacity for opening bazaars. A distinguished gentleman speaking at a recent bazaar opening in Carlisle, said it was impossible to say anything original on such occasions, and he (Mr. Allison) certainly did not intend to try and break the record. For his own part, he never could see why bazaars required opening. There seemed no place so easy to get into as bazaars or so difficult to get out of alive—that was so far as one's money was concerned. Inexorable custom, however, decreed that there must be an opening, and he hoped this bazaar would be a success. The object, the clearing off a debt upon the Wesleyan Sunday school, was one which would commend itself to them all. They all believed in the training of the children in the simple tenets of the Christian faith as the best preparation they could possibly have for their future career in life. If they wanted them to be good citizens in the future they must lead them in the right way when young. There were many points of connection between the Wesleyan body

E

Photo by   *F. Heyworth, St. Annes*

MYSELF AND LITTLE GIRL.

and the Church of England, which it was interesting to note. He would only mention one, in relation to the hymns and spiritual songs they sang. If they went into a Church of England place of worship, he ventured to say that, at a great many of their services, they would find them singing a hymn of John or Charles Wesleys'. On the other hand, if they went into a Wesleyan Church, he had no doubt they would occasionally find them singing hymns composed by distinguished members of the Church of England. This showed that there was a real bond of Christianity amongst them all. There were nothing like the hymns of the Church. To have written a good hymn conferred almost as much immortality upon one's name as if one had written Shakespeare. That hymn would be sung throughout all time, and once a spiritual sense was touched there was a bond of union that nothing could divide. He concluded with the expression of the hope that the result of the sale would be sufficient to liquidate the debt upon the school."

If our Swedenborgian friends are right in their views about Heaven, I may have the honour of meeting our ex-M.P. and ex-High Sheriff occasionally. The huge debt which had crippled our efforts in other directions having had decent burial, my thoughts diverted from bricks and mortar to the animated frames of human beings. I remember the lonely nights I put in in my native village. I remember the lonely hours I put in as minister in waiting on our old Ayreshire cow, when she was occupied with grazing on the road-sides. How few books were within my reach! A book always kept me quiet. What unearthly yells I let out when perched up the trees on the Howford Lonning! When the foliage was thick, how the startled passers by looked in vain to see where the voice proceeded from! As is well known, Hethersgill had earned an unenviable reputation for rowdyism at the time the people were going to its church or chapel on Sunday evenings. The most strenuous part of the parish policeman's duty came between six and seven o'clock on that day. I cannot say I ever blamed the lads very much. I always did, and do yet, like a bit of fun. The lads were lost for a little healthy recreation during the week, and a few kind words. Through my adverts. in the " East Cumberland News " I have published the wonderful fact that servant

Photo by **F. Heyworth**, *St. Annes.*

THE "SARK" M.P., AS "FATHER CHRISTMAS."

lads have souls. I was in Hethersgill during the Martinmas
Term Week in November, 1908. Where coersion had failed
I thought I would try a switch of kindness. Bob Mitchinson
bought me two hams for my feast. Mr. Harkress supplied
some special loaves, cakes, etc. Forty-five young men and
lads turned up as my guests. I see those sandwiches yet
in memory. Many of them passed out of sight the same
evening. The most ardent critic could not have complained
of their dimensions, especially in depth. No man or boy
managed to pass the fourth mile stone in sandwiches. Didn't
the lads grin when I asked them whether sandwiches or
policemen could catch them quicker! We nearly had an
all-night sitting, but we managed to adjourn the debate at
11-30. What a wonderful lecture they got on " Lessons
from John Hunt," the famous Fijian missionary, who started
work as a servant lad in Lincolnshire at the age of ten years.
Has any meeting of any description shown better behaviour
or greater interest in the theme before the House ? Has any
lecturer assumed a greater variety of attitudes in pouring
out such an appalling stream of eloquence whilst standing,
walking, sitting, or leaning ? The reading room idea was
carried without one opponent. The following evening, I was
favoured with the presence of the maiden ladies at our second
banquet edition. The night turned out stormy, so only 25
put in an appearance. I thought more of my female friends
might have turned up if their invitation had been fixed for
the first night also, but I wanted to blow the lads up by
themselves, that operation not being requisite in the suffragette
section of the North Cumberland Parliamentary Division.
The opening of Hethersgill reading room and recreation rooms,
on July 22nd, 1909, has been announced to the general public.
The visit of Madame Jessie Strathearn, A.R.A.M., has also
been notified. The wonderful out-burst of generosity which
supplied the temporal needs of over 500 hungry souls is also
a matter of history. Thirty members are now enrolled.
Party politics create no ill feeling. The " Daily Sketch "
and " Daily News " bring an outside village into touch with the
outside goings on in the world. The old bedroom that was
honoured with my presence, until leaving home, is now the
source of enjoyment for the lads. What memories are
associated with that little room ! What rows, as children,

THE REV. T. J. CHOATE.

we kicked up in it ! My father was nicknamed the Bishop
of Kirklinton. How often he laid his hand on my head and,
occasionally, on other parts of my body when I had got a
bit unmanagable. The reading room was our drawing,
reception, and best parlour all combined. The travelling
preachers were located in it for quietude and for tea-tasting
operations. My Methodist friends have not relished the new
innovation. My old friend and colleague, Mr. Teasdale,
does not see " eye to eye " with me. He thinks I am too
wide, and I think him too narrow. So we are both right.
Being miserable sinners in church and getting ready to die
in chapels do not furnish every thing in life. When will our
churches realise that our bodies want catering for as well
as our souls ? Times are altered. Education has shifted
many old landmarks that wanted removing. No gambling
or swearing is allowed. Few rooms can compare with them
for comfort. Few reading room committees possess the
same brains and discretion. Many village reading rooms
are closed through squabbles. I don't think Hethersgill
will reach that state. If it does, I shall still keep them open
as a place for the servant lads of the district. " The Rev.
T. J. Choate, ex-Chairman of the Liverpool District, will
visit the Reading Room on Saturday, July 23rd, and on
the following day preach in Penton Auction Mart at 2 o'clock,
and in Road Head Public Hall at 6-30."

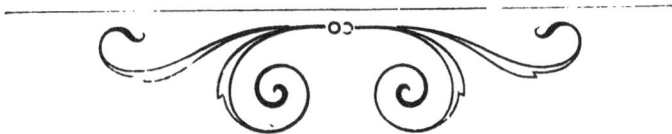

THESE SHEEP ARE PRESENTED BY THE CUMBERLAND FARMERS FOR THE LIQUIDATION OF THE DEBT ON HETHERSGILL CHAPEL AND SUNDAY SCHOOL SCHEME

John Heywood Ltd ,   Manchester.

MY BANNER FOR HETHERSGILL SHEEP FESTIVAL.

CHAPTER V.

FARMERS.

I HAVE referred so often in my newspaper adverts. to the farming community that this chapter can be easily curtailed. My farming experience finished before I reached the age of 16. Memory still carries one back to the times of harvest. What long hard days I have put in for the huge sum of one shilling ! What a struggle it was to raise the price of some new garment ! But they were happy days. There is even a difference in farmers. Some of them seemed satisfied with my performance, others thought a shilling a day should have produced more results to show for my labours. Mowing machines were not in universal use at the time. I never was weight to swing a scythe, but I managed to make bands ; and once, at West Knowe, my sister and I managed to " sheer " a rigg betwixt us ; my share being about one-third of the width of it. I think about the last of my harvesting operations took place at Prior Rigg ; Mr. Joshua Reay was farmer there. The old man did not smoke, but his sons did. It is wise to work where either master or sons smoke, if you want a little breathing space. I can still remember my old friends injunction to gather up " heads," Will. At the " Kern " supper he told me I was gathering up the heads quicker there than on the land. I still go back to my turnip-howing days at Broomhill. How Tom Calvert and I tried to turn our " hows " into brass instruments ! Such music we blew would have melted the heart of a stone. Nearly all the farms in Kirklinton have new tenants. Forty-two years has brought many changes. Perhaps no calling brings forth greater physical exertions than a farmers', but with all its disadvantages, a farmer's life has many points of advantage. A farmer seldom runs out of work. The boys soon come in to be useful, and the girls have splendid oppor-

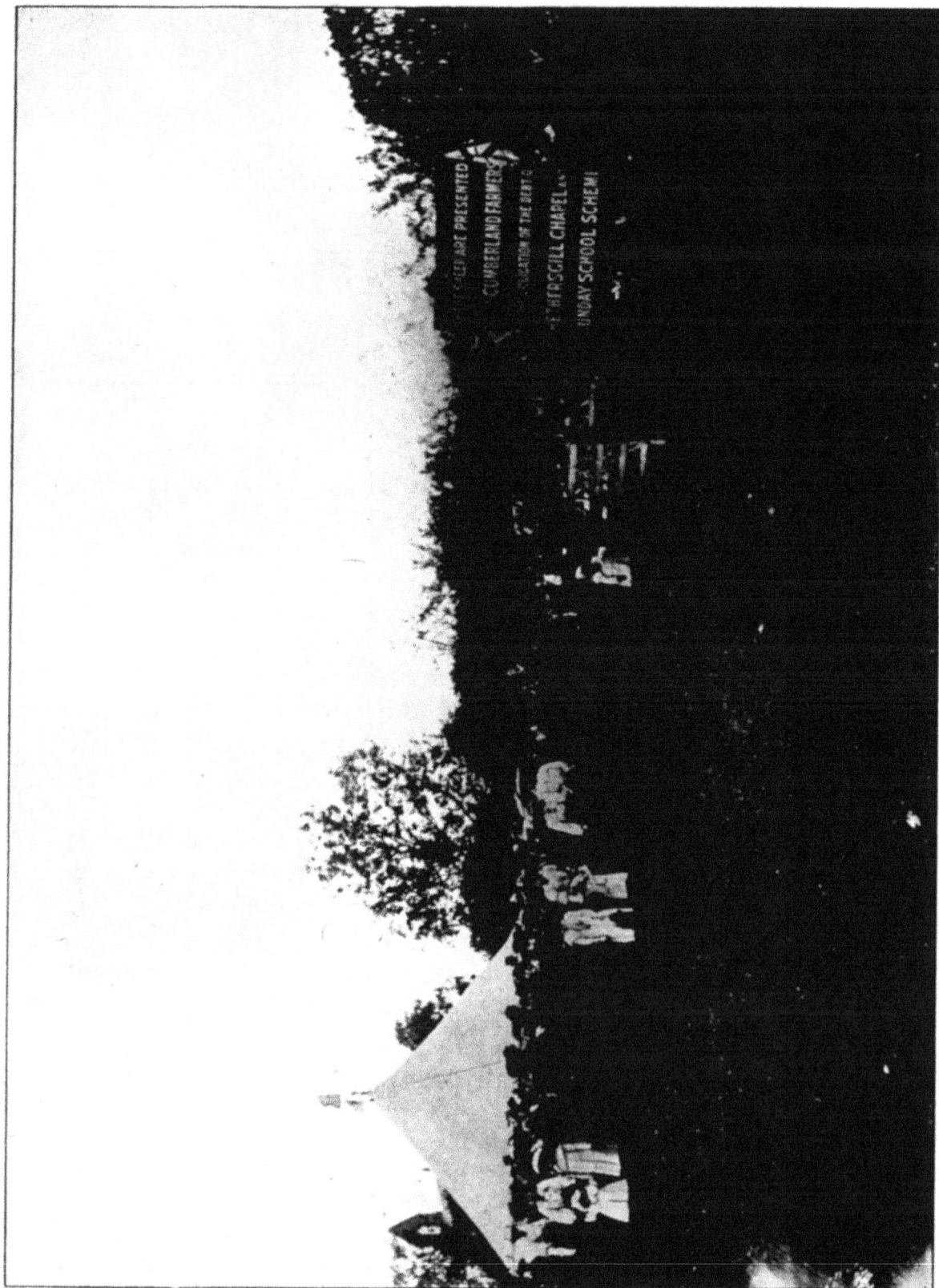

Photo by   R. B. Nicholson, Carlisle.

HETHERSGILL SHEEP FESTIVAL

tunities for developing healthy bodies ; as a class, I always think they stand highest. For nearly 20 years I travelled amongst them. I lost very little money amongst them, and I certainly never had a case for the County Court. The home influences are amongst the healthiest. The struggle to raise the rent develops habits of carefulness and thrift ; all the great forces in nature work silently. The finest and best traits of character are developed in the lonely homes. To me there is no more painful spectacles than the St. Annes' Promenade on Sunday evenings, and Scotch and English Streets, Carlisle, on the same nights. The aimless wanderings to and fro. The empty chatter, etc., etc. May I advise you to get your sons, as soon as possible, into business men ? It is wise for the father to stay at home and let the lads get their hands in at the auctions. My wife's shrewd old father once said to his younger son : " Jonathan, the purse is in that drawer, go and buy some bullocks. If you give too much for them, you will know better the next time." I know a few farmers' sons who are proper noodles through always having to stick at home. My two lads are doing most of the buying already. There is no more interesting work than farming. If a man has a love for nature, how nice to see the buds bursting forth. What is more interesting to watch than the lambs frisking round their mothers or running races in their playful way ? What more enjoyable work than trying to conquer the weeds in a field, and uproot all that may be detrimental to the growth of the coming crop ? I know some farmers who have a hard struggle to raise the rent, but they are wealthy men ; their upright conduct encourages uprightness in others. Their kindly consideration for others makes other folks respect them. The poor lad or lassie, who is driven by poverty from home to start work, is rich in circumstances who works for the man who has con-sideration for some other body's bairn. I know some wealthy farmers whose whole life and energies have been given to grasp and hoard money. Having got a lump, the lump is still craving for growth. Few tears will be shed at their funerals, unless they be tears of joy that the old miser has got out of the way at last, and the expectant relations have come in for the money that has cost its previous owner so dear.

MY SHEEP ON STANWIX BANK ON WAY TO AUCTION MART.

Photo by

R. B. Nicholson, Carlisle.

You will give my infirmary scheme thought. I want everybody to help. You may not be able to afford a sheep. A cock-duck from some of you may mean a more generous gift than a prize lamb from others. The Great Master looks more at the spirit of a gift than its actual value. He sees what we have left as well as what we " pairt " with. I hope the present generation of Cumberland farmers may leave such foot-prints on the sands of time that their sons will be better for trying to plant their feet on the same marks. May the sons, having a better start than their fathers had, keep going still higher up the scale and bring more blessing into Carlisle on the market days. What shall the harvest be ?

THE CUMBERLAND INFIRMARY.

Photo by

Beaven & Sons, Carlisle.

CHAPTER VI.

CARLISLE.

" Be just and fear not."

I MAKE no effort to deal with Carlisle from an historic standpoint ; that is already ancient history, and has been dealt with by much abler pens than mine. I have already expressed in plain and blunt terms, in my advertisements, my opinion of its present condition. I think no city can present greater difficulties for a new comer to make headway. Co-op. monopoly (credit amongst the so-called better class), country travelling, clannishness, etc., etc., all unite to call forth extra exertion from the man who wants to push his way. I have often expressed my admiration for the northern environment of our city. It is well to have good prospects, both in landscapes and other things ; unfortunately, good prospects do not represent present assets. I knew the city was limp and depressed before my coming to it. I came back to Carlisle to once more resume business operations with my old customers, as Carlisle is the gathering ground for them. In its present condition rents are certainly far too high, and the rates are in the same condition. There is no city for position, I know of, that can compare with it ; but as Carlisle is living on its past history, we are paying a big price to be respectable. After a long experience of the throb of Manchester life the contrast is a great one betwixt the two cities, so my opinions may be thought a bit too harsh to those who have spent most of their lives in our sleepy city. From a manufacturing standpoint, Carlisle is placed at a great disadvantage through being too far away from Lancashire. The margin of profit is cut down so close that time and carriage make that margin still smaller. Having some practical knowledge of London, Liverpool, and other of our large cities, I think Manchester stands pre-eminent for the tone of its business spirit. The former mentioned cities may present more refinement, but blunt, unpolished Lancashire and Yorkshire manufacturers control the pulse of the greatest and strongest fibres in the world's productions. I write in no carping spirit of criticism ; the present and future condition of Carlisle must certainly cause serious reflection to any one with the soul and brains to grasp the

CARLISLE.—FROM THE NORTH APPROACH.

position. I think Carlisle's greatest enemies could not charge it with being overburdened with pluck. Northerners are generally credited with the faculty of being able to look after the " baw-bees." I think other parts of England have caught the same spirit. Many of the last generation of Carlisle tradesmen were once country lads who came to the city to make money. It does not take a very brilliant man, who lives solely for the purpose of acquiring money, to get hold of it. Unfortunately, the pursuit of it largely warps the best instincts of his nature. The yellow fever getting into his brains he sticks to the gold, without helping or blessing the best interests of the place where his money is made. When the time limit has expired, such men die bankrupt. As a rule, infirmaries, hospitals, and other beneficent institutions do not figure heavily in his list of legacies. The wealth is largely left to the family. What is more paralysing to the energies of most men than having money left to them? The

THE COURT HOUSE AND GAOL, CARLISLE.

sweets of hard work, by brain and hands, are denied them. What a blessing it would be to plenty of Carlisle's present tradesmen if the money their fathers left to them would take to its self wings and fly away! I think the annual report of the Cumberland Infirmary, Carlisle, may be taken as a fair test of the generosity and philanthropy of the Upper Ten class of Carlisle. How often the magnificent donation of £2 2s. appears after the names of some of the richest men in Carlisle! I think the present financial condition of an institution that should appeal to all sections and sects alike is simply disgraceful. The influence of a cathedral in a small

F

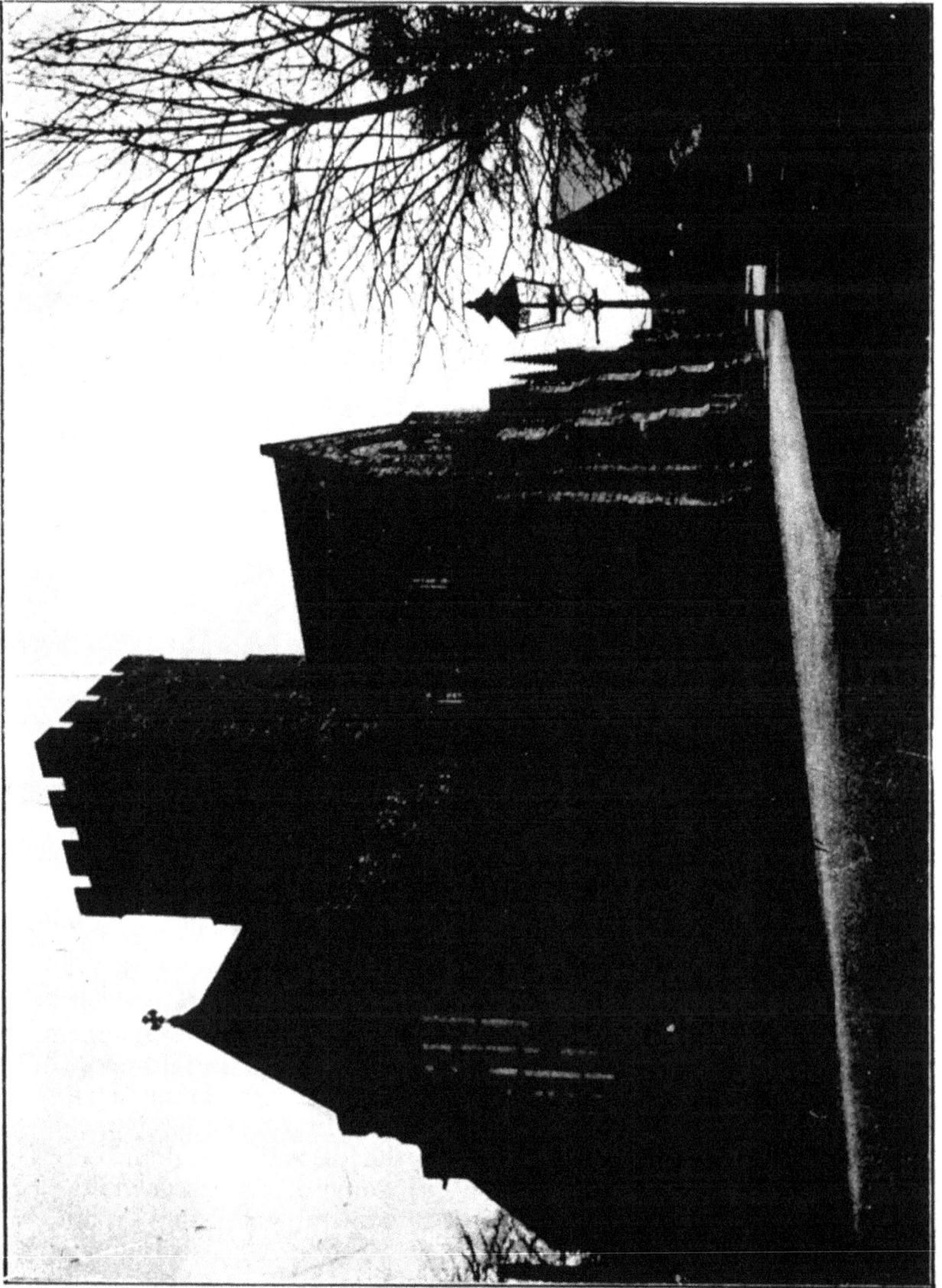

THE CATHEDRAL, CARLISLE.

Country city is also not helpful to an aggressive spirit, which these strenuous times demand. Carlisle is suffering from the dry rot of respectability. I make no complaint of cathedral services. Some cultured souls will get to heaven through culture. Whether is Carlisle Cathedral services or the Church Army doing most for Carlisle ? The true spirit of Christianity is self-sacrifice. Are the attendants at our Cathedral services trying to uplift Carlisle ? That is the most practical test.

Having spent the best part of my life in trying to help Methodism, I am sorry I am in rather bad repute in some Methodist circles. What does the monument to the Rev. Geo. Latham mean near the Skating Rink ? The Rev. Geo. Latham and myself are both men who have got monuments erected to their memory whilst still living. Bob Addison erected mine when he put up the stone pillars in the entrance to my orchard at Hethersgill. There is room for the inscription, " He was a good beggar " on one of the gate-posts.

From a trade standpoint I think my advent into Carlisle has been helpful to it. I wonder how much more the Crown and Mitre Buildings would realise to-day than the amount they would have done if offered for sale before my tenancy of two of its shops ? My " Sark " family have been good friends to me. How widely divergent have been the opinions expressed about my designation of shirts !

My first advert. in the " East Cumberland News " caught on. My eight illustrations created attention and comment all over Cumberland. Many friends and well-wishers were not sparing in their condemnation of my using, what they called, a vulgar word. Everybody has a right to their own ideas and opinions. I have noticed that where condemnation was strongest patronage has been weakest. " Sarks " have done well for me, and are doing well for my customers. It is a lucky hit when we can catch a phrase that will stick. Through calling them " Sarks " I am sending shirts all over Cumberland, Westmorland, Northumberland, and Dumfries-shire. For size, quality, and finish my " Sarks " stand without a rival. I don't think that either my friends or foes can charge me with sticking to old ruts. Corn sheaves were seen wearing men's " Sarks " in Carlisle for the first time. Turnips, potatoes, and other vegetables took the

INTERIOR OF CARLISLE CATHEDRAL.

place of different classes of drapery goods at my " Sark " harvest festival. I have had myself transformed into " Father Christmas," and have had the honour to present a small article, ranging in value from one penny to 2s. 11d. each, to hundreds of children at Penton, Roadhead, Roweltown, and Southwaite. There is no need to be orthodox about the 25th of December. This has been a good mode of advertising, and given pleasure both to the bairns and the parents of the bairns. I do not expect to make a large fortune in Carlisle, and I am not going to try. I have seen too many samples of what were once decent kind of men turned into land sharks through the demoralising worship of gold. I have not been, what the world usually terms, a successful man of business I could have been if I had had the same appetite for mor that is characteristic of the ordinary type of retail master drapers. No apprentice could have a poorer pasture than I had. Having several shops, and my two lads not showing any particular bent for any other trade or profession, they have followed in my footsteps as regards a trade. I sent them away to other towns to serve their apprenticeships. The older lad was lucky in the food department ; the younger one shared my fate. I have had other folks' bairns as my apprentices, but I defy any of them to complain of meanness on my part. How many hundreds and thousands of country lads have been thrown into consumption through insufficient diet at the time of life they most need propping. I am glad that Carlisle drapers have good repute amongst travellers. A London commercial told my lad that with the exception of one town, Carlisle drapers are the nicest lot of men he calls upon. The traveller has not seen me yet, otherwise I might reduce the average, and be the cause of changing his opinion. I shall not make a huge fortune now, but I don't think I shall ever become a permanent visitor to any of our workhouses.

I still possess the old parental cottages at Hethersgill. Mr. Millican, Scotby, has planted me 42 apple trees, 12 Victoria plum trees, and a quantity of gooseberry trees, so as I can live rent free ; and if I can manage to buy a stone of flour occasionally I am safe for a Girdle cake or a " bit apple dumpling." I shall do alright. I have got my two lads fixed up in healthy environments ; they have had a better start in life than I had, so they can live if they stick in.

Photo by   THE BUTTER MARKET, CARLISLE.   *R. B. Nicholson, Carlisle.*

CHAPTER VII.

MY SCHEME FOR CLEARING THE DEBT ON THE CHILDREN'S
" PAIRT " OF THE CUMBERLAND INFIRMARY.

As I have already spent a good amount in ventilating this scheme in my advertisements in the " East Cumberland News," my last chapter can be a brief one.

Although the Methodist Church carries the palm for raising money by every conceivable and unconceivable method, I have yet to meet my marrow for patience, perseverance, and ingenuity in the art of extracting subscriptions. It is, perhaps, as well that this gift is not general. I must admit, however, that Hethersgill chapel scheme exhausted all the sources that I could contrive or invent. Roweltown Chapel was re-opened, after thorough renovation, on April 25th. The whole debt was cleared by the following October, although I raised more than half myself. After the second strenuous effort for Hethersgill, I had a serious nervous breakdown, which lasted a considerable while. Going to live at St. Annes, the change set me up. I went in March, and when, in the following May, I found I could write a begging letter again, I knew I had got better. In a fortnight I got over £40, and this amount was all from previous subscribers. Then my wonderful Harvest Sheep Festival Scheme broke upon me. It was a grand idea, and a grand and original scheme. Had I been able to spare the time to go round the farmers, I think I should have got as many sheep given as would have freed the chapel and Sunday school from debt. In an evil hour the idea of giving prizes wrecked the scheme. The purity of motive was taken out of it. The offer of prizes stopped many farmers from giving anything. I am quite certain no local agricultural society in Cumberland ever offered such an array of valuable articles. From June to October I practically gave the whole of my time to the scheme.

Telegrams
"CHAMPNESS, LUTTERWORTH"

(Manchester)

Lutterworth,

2 Oct 1905

Mr W Moffitt

My dear friend,

I dont know whether I am most amused or amazed at your literature It would be a good thing if the Tutors would allow you to give an address to the Students at the various colleges Such "Horse sense" as the Yankees call it is not often found.

I do hope that you will be well supported by the farming interest. My purse is not what it used to be but if you want an odd 10/- you will know where to find it

The other day I spent a day with Mr Smart. how grows on me now does that man. He is a saint of the first water

Best of luck to you

Thomas Champness

[margin:] Remember me to the Teasdale folk &c

From 5 o'clock in the mornings until after midnight I was engaged in sending out the most beautiful lot of circulars I have ever seen. The originality of the idea caught the eye of the Press. Many of the most influential and smartest newspapers in England made reference to the scheme. The American newspapers copied it. Several magazines, such as the "Sunday Circle," inserted articles and copied the illustrations. I collected £64 10s. 9d., the whole of which was given away in prizes. McDougall's, of sheep dipping fame, spontaneously offered a complete set of sheep dipping utensils. I had given my labour, brain power, etc., and finished up be being £50 poorer in purse than when I started. Never has such a crowd been gathered in Hethersgill as on the great day. Never so much cry—never so little wool. I could not rest with the failure, so I rigged myself up with a water-proof outfit and faced the angry elements in a bleak November. I borrowed traps, and I hired traps, and drove round the outlying districts. All the lambs being sold, I begged for the following year. Then I saw where I had ruined my scheme. Lots of decent farmers, who would have given such sheep as they possessed, told me they had nothing fit to show. In a fortnight I had got a provisional promise of nearly 60 sheep, to be collected the following September. The superhuman strain brought on another collapse during the following February. When September came there was no one to collect my sheep. The letter from a rabid vegetarian killed the local sheep collecting enthusiasm (if there was any), and the weary debt hung on.

Three Septembers passed away. I was still unfit for any further exertion. In August, 1908, I had three courses open to me for a holiday: To go with a friend to Zeebrugge; to go to Keswick Convention; or to go and visit the friends who has promised a sheep (which had not been called for), and see if their promises would still be fulfilled. It was weary work, as I was in poor form.

Brampton Wesleyans had just held a large and successful bazaar. The friends in Bewcastle had another in connection with their Public Hall at Roadhead. Smithfield Mission Room had also sprung into existence. I was strongly advised to wait another year. The apathy of the friends most concerned gave me the chance to get better.

Photo by F. Heyworth, St. Annes.

Let me tell any friend who may be suffering from nervous depression that the cure rests in your own hands. My doctor at St. Annes told me, If I would put myself into his hands, he would cure me in three months. Without the aid of a doctor I cured myself in a week at Hethersgill. Bob Mitchinson sent his son with me in his long market trap. We put a pig-net over it. We started at Horsgill's and finished at Moss Thorn. Having changed horses at noon, I collared anything that had life in it, or that had no life in it, if it could be made into money. I got sheep, hens, ducks, pigeons, etc. I got 26 lambs of different dimensions, and got them sold at Hetherington's cattle and sheep sale at Boltonfell End. If I had thrown money away at my first effort, not a single penny was spent that could be avoided. The auctioneer kindly sold them free from commission. As I left the Auction Mart and turned my foot-steps towards Hethersgill the gloom that had hung over me for three years lifted once more, and I have not given it a chance to return. Most people will think I have had enough of sheep schemes. I have, for the Hethersgill Chapel, as the debt is off. If the country people keep our shop doors open in Carlisle, it will be the farmers and other country people who can clear the debt off the Children's Ward in our Infirmary.

Most country people are lost for having some object to interest them. There is not a lonely farm house or village but shall have something now to go at. My sheep scheme may be a bit stiff in the joints this year, but it will go and get better and easier to work and produce more interest and enthusiasm every year. It will be most interesting to the farmers to set a lamb aside every year, and watch it growing. The farmers' wives will pay special attention to the cock-duck or hen-drakes. We will all profit by my blunders. Some of the servant lads will be clubbing together to buy and send a lamb. The servant lasses can concoct something to help. If we all bend our backs and use our brains the financial result will surprise everybody next September, and no one more so than the Treasurer of the Cumberland Infirmary. I shall profit by the financial failure of my first annual concert. Last year I sent £50 to the Treasurer, and lost another £30 in working expenses. I'll cut down the expenses this year. All my artistes shall have the honour and pleasure of giving

MOFFITT BROS. CASH DRAPERS

WE SELL AT ONE PRICE TO EVERYBODY

Photo by   *F. Heyworth, St. Annes.*

MY DRAPERY SHOP, ST. ANNES.

their services. We shall go in for local merit to shine. My professional friends, who did so well last year, shall have to cross their names off my list. I will keep the price of tickets down ; one shilling is plenty for a concert these dull times.

Now I am finished. I may have set " pairt " of my book more than once. I have nothing " set " to keep me right, as my manuscript has been sent off to the printer in sections. What will be the verdicts on my book ? No praise shall turn my head. No censure shall cause any loss of sleep. Is the capital " I " the source of my literary efforts ? Is the " Sale of Sarks " the purest philanthropy represented ? Everybody can have their own opinion about it. If I have struck a chord in any heart, let us all try to do a bit to brighten our " pairt " of the world, and if it is given a chance " Canny old Cumberland will cap them a still."

Photo by　　　　　　　　　　　　　　　　　　Porthouse, Carlisle.

Photo by   MY DRAPERY SHOP, No. 12, ENGLISH STREET, CARLISLE.

Porthouse, Carlisle.

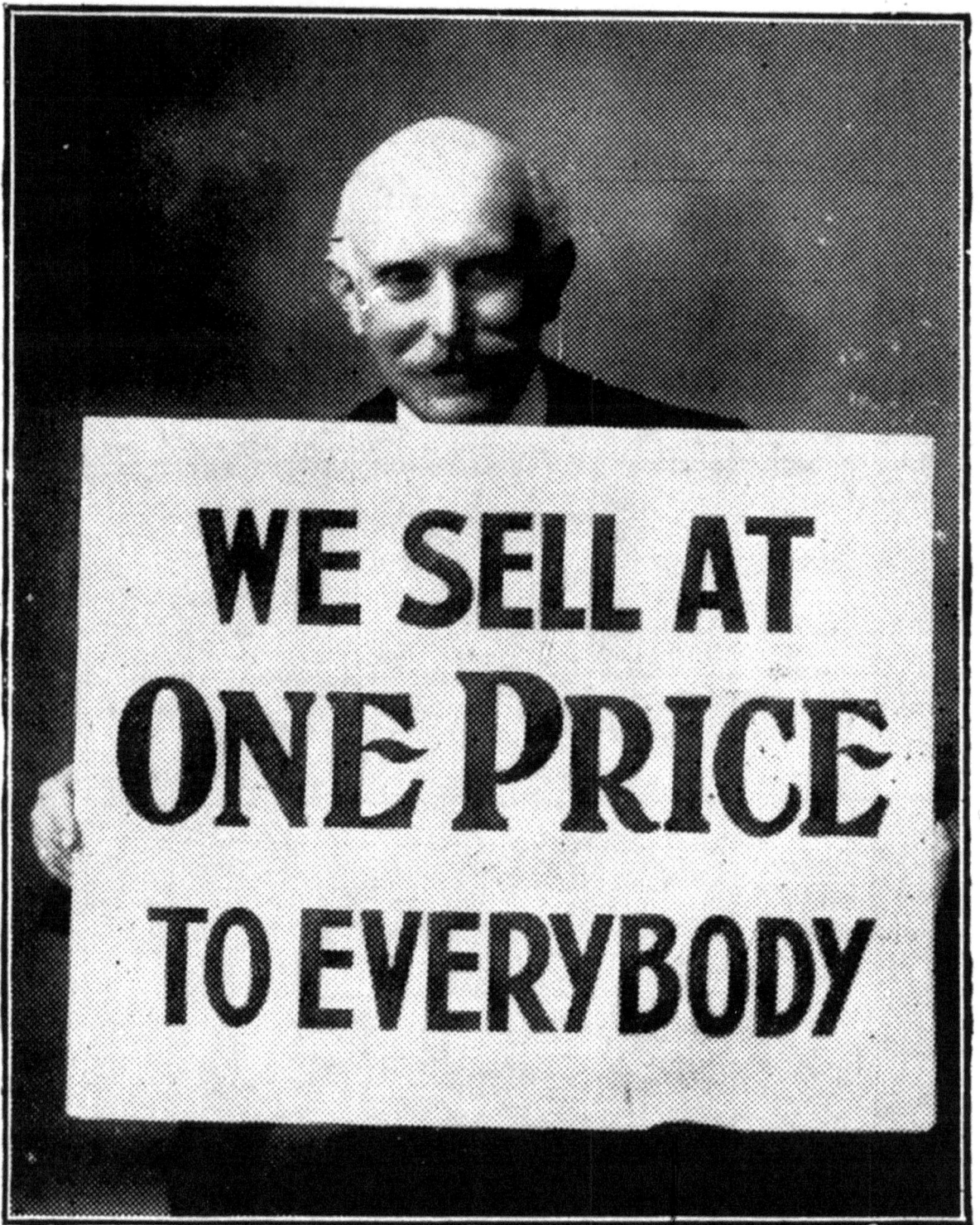

Photo by   *F. Heyworth, St Annes.*

EVERY THING AT LOWEST CASH PRICES.